TRAINING OTHERS TO READ GOD'S WORD

MATT ROGERS

Training Others to Read God's Word
©2016 by Matt Rogers
ISBN 978-0-9973993-0-1

Unless otherwise noted, all Biblical references used in this book were taken from The Holy Bible, English Standard Version ® (ESV ®) Copyright © 2001 by Crossway, a publishing ministry of Good News Publishers. All rights reserved.

Printed in the United States of America.

For those who pastor God's Church–

AN INTRODUCTION TO PASTOR FIELD NOTES

There's a long way between a seminary classroom and a pastor's desk. Whether you've been to seminary, read a few books, or just have a burning passion to serve God's church, it does not take long to realize that there is more to the task of pastoral ministry than most assume.

My on-ramp to pastoral ministry was convoluted to say the least. I loved Jesus and His church, and before I knew it, I was on staff in a local church. I had no clue what I was doing—a fact that was confirmed on an almost daily basis. Though I was given ample opportunity to lead, I was not trained to care for God's people in the local church. I took a few seminary classes, but lacked any intentional plan to develop my theological insight or my practical ministry skills. In the years that followed, I preached sermons, taught Bible study classes, led mission trips, and organized ministry activities, but ministry growth consisted of the painful process of trial and error. I'd do something, it wouldn't work, so I'd do something else. I longed to be a good pastor and felt that the Spirit had given me the rudimentary skills for doing so, but I needed training, and I knew it.

A decade later I arrived at Southeastern Baptist Theological Seminary in Wake Forest, North Carolina. There I met godly professors and fellow students who were passionate about God, His word, and His work in the world. I learned lofty theological truths, hermeneutical paradigms, historical realities, and missiological principles that have shaped my ministry to this day. But, my learning extended far beyond the seminary. In fact, my most effective training happened, not in the seats of a seminary classroom, but in the day-to-day life of the local church.

By God's grace, our family joined one of a number of healthy local churches near the seminary, and there we found pastors who not only rightly communicated the glorious gospel, but also lived lives that were transformed by God's grace and gave time to training future leaders for the church. It was in the local church that I was forced to apply the doctrine I learned in the classroom to the real-life work of leading God's church. I found that it is far easier to define a proper homiletical method than it is to preach a good sermon. It is far easier to write a position paper on divorce and remarriage than it is to counsel a couple experiencing the horror of a marriage on the brink of disaster. It is fascinating to consider the contextual realities shaping missions and evangelism in the modern world, but frustrating to apply those same realities to sharing the gospel with a neighbor or co-worker. The local church gave me a context that forced me to practice James' principle by living as a doer of the word and not merely a hearer (Jam 1:22).

Within local church ministry, I soon learned that there are all sorts of things you have to do that are hard to find in the normal books we were reading. As a novice pastor, I was mesmerized by the depth of theological insight found in many of the books I was assigned. My shelves are filled with many of these works, which bear the marks to prove the impact they had on my life. Often the stated goal and extensive reach of these books caused the authors to write on a macro-level. They sought to defend broad theological principles, argue for precise doctrinal claims, or establish universal definitions of the nature and mission of the church. In these books, I found a firm place for my feet to rest and from which to do ministry.

Yet, I wanted and needed more. I needed books that could help me put feet to the theology they professed. I needed humble pastors who could take the "whats" and "whys" and give me some guidance on "how". I needed authors who could take the final two-sentences of application found in their chapters and tease these out into a more extensive guide for young guys like me.

That is my modest goal in *Pastor's Notes*. I write as a blue-collar theologian who loves to help pastors navigate the complexity of vocational ministry.

These small books are meant to be practical guides on a host of standard pastoral issues. For this reason, they will all be incomplete. I make no effort to provide robust theological foundations, assuming that other scholars are far better equipped than I to undertake this vital task. I'll choose to build off of the work of great thinkers and apply their insight to guide ministers in a host of practical issues ranging from teaching the church to read the Bible, raising money, training lay leaders to provide pastoral care, developing a Constitution and Bylaws, organizing teams of lay leaders, and a host of other topics. By writing them as individual books, my intention is that these concise guides are short enough to be read in one or two sittings and are easy to read with a team of elders, deacons, staffs, or interns.

The wedding of theology and practice is vital for the health of God's church. My prayer is that these *Pastor's Notes* make a helpful contribution to guide current and future pastors to steward the glorious gift we've been entrusted—the bride of Christ—the local church.

Matt

TRAINING OTHERS TO READ GOD'S WORD

How'd he do that? The thought was almost audible. I remember listening to a preacher teach a familiar passage on the radio while sitting in my green Ford Ranger pickup in the parking lot at Furman University. I had read the same text many times since my conversion due to my seemingly insatiable hunger for God's word. Yet, hearing this skilled pastor proclaim the Scriptures brought out a depth of meaning and beauty that I didn't see when reading the Bible alone.

Honestly, I was stunned and frustrated. Why hadn't I seen that? What was he doing that allowed him to notice nuances and complexities of the Scripture that I did not? Would it require a seminary degree to be able to read the Bible, understand its meaning, and apply it to my life?

Now, as a pastor of a local church who writes and preaches regularly, I hear people ask me those questions. They share how a sermon has challenged, convicted, or spurred them on to spiritual maturity. They talk about how God used his proclaimed word to show them truth they'd been missing for years. And for that I am thankful.

I am also scared. I am afraid that I may subtly create a chasm between myself and the people who sit in the seats each Sunday. I am frightened that they may depend on me for too much. I am scared that this may produce passivity in them, thinking that somehow I am doing something they will never be able to do. And, I am convicted that my God-given role is to equip God's saints for the work of the ministry which most certainly means that I have a responsibility to teach them to feast on God's word for themselves (Eph 4:11–16).

Certainly, everyone who attends the local church that I pastor will not stand before large groups of people and teach the Scriptures regularly. Some will. Most will not. What they will do is awaken every day with a treasure sitting on a shelf in their house—the treasure of God's revealed word. *What they do with their Bible will shape the trajectory of their lives.*

Of the myriad of practical challenges pastors face in equipping their people to walk with Jesus faithfully, their greatest feat is training believers to read God's word well. Anyone who has pastored a church for any length of time can attest to the fact that far too many believers lack either the discipline to meet with God in his word or a plan to do so with intentionality and skill. We may teach expository sermons each week or even hand out a Bible reading plan at the first of the year, yet fail to equip our people to read, understand, and apply the Bible themselves.

The equipping process demands that pastors develop a plan of attack when it comes to teaching others to read the Bible well. That's why I developed Seven Arrows. God was gracious to allow me to plant a new church in Greenville, South Carolina in the summer of 2009. God brought many spiritually immature people to our congregation, and we set out on the long journey to make disciples.

God was at work in the lives of many in our congregation and, as a result, they had a deep hunger to know God through his word. I knew they were reading the Bible and truly seeking to hear from God and obey what he said. But they were new to the Bible—or at least new to actually caring about what the Bible had to say. Many sat in churches as children, left as teenagers, and were just now reengaging with the truths of the gospel. These people were not theology students—they were average college juniors, homeschool moms, or business professionals who wanted to meet with God through his word.

As a pastor, I had options at this point. I could give them a thick hermeneutics textbook and encourage them to read on their own. If I gave them a thick book of theological principles I knew that it would only heighten the insecurities of those who were new to God's word.

I could put them in a class where they would be taught these same principles. But I knew that the classroom setting is challenging for many people—particularly new believers. They feel ill-equipped to keep up with the maturity and insight of others who are in the class. They may also hesitate to ask the questions they have as they read to avoid looking bad in front of others.

Or, I could give him another author's reflections on the Bible. Don't get me wrong, devotional guides are necessary and helpful tools for the church; however, most people need to start with the Bible rather than training themselves to depend on someone else to do the work for him. If I simply handed them another devotional guide, I would be doing the same thing that I wanted to avoid in my preaching—I would be teaching them to depend on a middleman to help them read the Bible.

THE SEVEN ARROWS

There's no magic in the Seven Arrows. As I'll explain later, any number of methods can be effective and helpful for teaching others to read the Bible well. What is important is that you have a plan—and that you use it regularly.

The first time I doodled the Seven Arrows I had no intention of building a model that would help churches read the Bible. I was simply trying to disciple one young man in our church. He was saved, baptized, and given his first Bible, which he read regularly. We met each week to talk about what he was reading, and in the context of that relationship, I saw the need to develop a tool like the Seven Arrows.

As I continued to meet with this guy, I sketched directional arrows that I thought might help him read the Bible in a clear and logical order and would help him see the big idea that God, through the biblical authors, was trying to communicate. I reflected on my own process of Bible study—both in my personal quiet time and in my sermon preparation each week—and tried to list the questions I asked about the biblical text.

I started with Arrow 1—this circular arrow that wraps around itself, making a dot. Arrow 1 asks, *What does this passage say?*

My goal was to get the reader to summarize what they'd just read in a simple, succinct sentence or two. By restating the text in their own words, the reader is able to process the passage and clarify its intended meaning in their minds. The person may be reading a sentence or a small paragraph, making the answer to Arrow 1 fairly straightforward; however, they might be reading a parable of Jesus, a longer chapter in the historical section of the Old Testament, or one of Paul's notoriously long run-on sentences. These passages need a little more work to summarize in simple idea. The answer to this question propels the reader forward—as the remaining six Arrows can be used to check to see if their main idea was God's main idea.

From there, Arrow 2 was a backward pointing arrow that asked, *What did this passage mean to its original audience?*

This question forces the reader to consider the biblical context and avoid rushing into personalized application in the modern context. God empowered the biblical author to record a text for a certain audience at a certain time in history. This is no accident. By considering what the original hearers or readers would have understood from a section of Scripture, modern readers are better positioned to make application for their lives as well. In order to answer this question well, the reader will have to consult study notes in their Bible itself or supplementary resources like Bible dictionaries, commentaries, or online resources. This process allows a pastor to train his people to understand how to access these helpful resources that many Bible readers squander on a regular basis. Such an understanding of the biblical text will allow the reader to see depth of meaning and application they might otherwise miss. For example, a reader who knows the Pharisees normative response to Jesus may understand certain responses by Jesus would have provoked their hatred all the more. Or, a reader who understood the deep-seated hostility between the Jews and Samaritans, and the low view of women during this time, may notice how provocative Jesus' interaction with the Samaritan woman at the well in John 4 would have been to his disciples.

Arrow 3 asks, *What does this passage tell us about God?*

The Trinitarian God of the Bible is the main character of every passage. Each page of the Bible is filled with testimonies to the nature and character of God and his work in the world. Some passages reveal more about God the Father, others the work of the Holy Spirit, and still others the person and work of Jesus Christ. The third Arrow forces the Bible reader to begin with God, and not man, at the heart of the biblical narrative. The glory of God and the brilliance of his mission to save sinners through the person and work of Jesus lay the foundation for a proper understanding of the gospel and the way in which we should respond to this great God.

Next, the reader is asked to consider the question: *What does this passage tell us about man?*

Here the reader must grapple with the way the text demonstrates the fallen, sinful condition of all people by virtue of their inherited sin nature apart from the gracious intervention of God. Bible readers may also notice the way the text reveals the transformation God brings to those whom he saves through the power of his Holy Spirit. Humans are not all that creative in our sin, so the actions, themes, and idolatry we see among the nation of Israel or the broken churches of the New Testament should hold up a mirror that exposes our own sin as well.

From there, the reader is ready to answer the question that often gets the most attention by Bible readers: *What does this passage demand of me?*

We are all prone to read the Bible with this question at the forefront due to our proclivity to place ourselves at the heart of the biblical narrative and not God. We may also erroneously believe that the Bible is a guidebook for moral people to learn how to navigate life. This leads to all sorts of distortions of the Bible's wisdom and we might rip the passage from its biblical context and apply it in an unclear, unhelpful, or incorrect way; however, with the context of Arrows 1–4 in place, the reader is now positioned to make personal application from the text properly. Now that the reader can summarize the passage in its historical context, describe the way the passage reveals the nature and actions of God, and explain how it exposes the sinful propensities of humans apart from the grace of God, they are then positioned to make proper application. This application will target the head (what the person believes), the heart (what they love), or the hands (how they act). Each facet of obedience is critical for effective application of God's word.

Arrow 6 stresses the corporate application of the biblical text. The Christian faith and the Bible are meant to be understood within the community of the church and in the context of mission to the world. The application of the demands of Arrow 5 will be embodied in relationships to other people. As a result, Arrow 6 asks the reader to consider, *How does this passage change the way I relate to people?*

This question makes overt the reality that virtues like love or humility, or actions like evangelism or generosity, require interaction with others. The communal application of the word allows the local church community to pulsate with attentiveness and transformation derived from God's word. It also fosters a missional spirit that prompts the reader to consider how the application of the Bible fuels their love for the lost and their mission to the nations.

Finally, Arrow 7—and all effective Bible reading—ends with prayer. Following the path outlined by the Arrows allows these prayers to be informed and based on God's word rather than merely on human needs and desires. Bible readers can pray, thanking God for his character that they've observed in the passage of Scripture. Or, they can confess sin in their lives because they've seen these same sins in the lives of those in the Bible. Readers might also pray, asking God to empower them to obey the application they've derived by asking the questions posed by Arrows five and six. So, we conclude by asking: *What does this text prompt me to pray?*

Asking this question is a proper way to end time spent in God's word and allows for prayers that are informed, sustained, and amplified by a right understanding of God as seen in the Bible.

That's it. I formulated a simple process that would aid my brother in reading the Bible for himself, understanding the intended meaning, and applying that meaning to his life. I never intended these simple doodles to go beyond that breakfast table. But they have.

Disciples of Jesus are hungry for simple, practical tools to aid them in knowing God and making him known. I have watched disciple-makers in our church use these Arrows to help a new believer grow in faith and understanding. I have watched teenagers read the Bible for themselves and unearth deep and profound truths of God's word. I have watched missionaries in other countries translate and use these Arrows to aid in mission to unreached parts of the world. In fact, we've been blessed to see many missionaries translate the simple bookmark we designed using these Arrows into the other languages so that pastors and disciple-makers can train others to read the Bible well. You can find examples of these bookmarks on our website at www.sevenarrowsbible.com.

Finally, I have seen other churches take these Arrows and use them to shape a disciple-making culture in their church, proving that it is possible for church members to be faithful in the task of studying the Bible and making disciples. The widespread hunger for practical tools like the Seven Arrows reveals the hunger that pastors and congregations have for practical tools to aid them in their disciple-making mission. These tools foster the type of mission we long to be embodied in our churches and reproduced through church planting and international missions. These plans are not an arbitrary extra to add to the otherwise full plate that pastors already have—they are vital if we hope to fulfill the Great Commission in our day.

WHY PLANS MATTER

I have yet to meet a pastor who would say, "You know, I'm really not that interested in whether or not my congregation reads their Bibles. I'm fine with them coming to church once or twice a week and hearing a solid sermon. That's all the Bible they need."

No one worthy of the title of "pastor" would say something so naïve and foolish. We tell people that they need to spend daily, consistent time meeting with God in His word. This, we say, is the key to maturing in the faith and growing in godliness. We are often stunned when we learn the unfortunate reality: *most people simply don't read their Bibles very much.*

The reasons for lack of Bible reading in our churches could be traced to many sources: difficulty understanding the Bible, spiritual apathy, the modern pace of life, or a host of other factors. While these may be true, I believe there is another possible culprit and one that pastors can, and should, do something about. *Many people don't read the Bible because they don't know how.*

It is entirely possible for people to come to church gatherings week after week, know that they need to read the Bible, and fail to do so because they've never been equipped to read the Bible well.

The task of equipping the church lies at the heart of pastoral ministry. Paul, in Ephesians 4, writes that God gives leaders to the church for the purpose of "equipping the saints" (Eph 4:11–16). This task is central to the mission that is given to every pastor, church planter, small group leader, youth minister, and anyone else who serves to lead the local church. We are to work diligently to ensure that the people whom God has entrusted to our care are equipped with the tools to aid them in obeying the commands of Christ as an act of worship.

Bible reading presents a wonderful case study as to whether or not a church leader is being faithful to their equipping task. It is possible to write good sermons, teach faithful Bible study class, run a host of programs and fail to equip anyone to read the Bible for themselves. *While our active teaching says "You should read your Bible" we may passively communicate "I don't care if you read the Bible" if we do help them know how to read the Bible well.*

To do this we need a plan. I know. . . I know. . . You don't like plans. It feels so programmed, so dry, so forced. Just tell people to do it and let them figure it out for themselves. This laissez-faire attitude is largely responsibly for the massive Biblical illiteracy that plagues our churches. Most people do not figure it out themselves. They may try hard for a few days, but then they get discouraged and simply give up.

While we may all shun stale programs or packaged systems, it is vital to develop a clearly organized plan for training people how to read the Bible well. There is no one-size-fits-all method for accomplishing this goal. What is important is that we have a plan.

Some churches utilize the S.O.A.P. method (www.soapstudy.com) to accomplish this goal. The acronym stands for:

- <u>S</u>cripture – First, people are instructed to read the passage of Scripture
- <u>O</u>bservation – Then, they were told to observe things in the passage that stood out
- <u>A</u>pplication – Third, they were to apply the passage to their lives
- <u>P</u>rayer – Finally, they were to pray in light of what they had seen in the passage that day

I found this to be a wonderfully helpful way of teaching people how to read the Bible. The Seven Arrows is another model, similar in many ways to the S.O.A.P method. The first four arrows help the reader accomplish the task of observation, arrows 5-6 aid in applying the text, and arrow seven concludes with prayer. We have found Bible readers are helped when they are given additional specifics as to what to observe and apply as they read the Bible.

For some, the S.O.A.P acronym will work best. Others will thrive using the Inductive Bible Study method, while others may find that the Seven Arrows is a useful tool. What is important is that each church strives to find something that works best and uses that method to disciple its people in the hopes that the knowledge and skills acquired will last for the rest of our lives.

MARKS OF A GOOD PLAN

Everyone in my house is constantly singing and I hate it. I blame my wife who is currently homeschooling our three children and participating in a Classical Conversations community. For those unfamiliar with this thrill-ride, everything (and I do mean everything) they are learning is set to song. History sentences, math problems, and science lessons all come with a cute jingle, memorable for young and old alike. In one song, which if I am not mistaken takes 13-minutes to sing, you can recount the entire timeline of world history with corresponding hand motions for each significant fact.

As annoying as this process may be, I can attest to the fact that my kids are learning things now that I do not know to this day. They don't learn it for a moment to pass a test, either, they remember those silly songs forever. And so will I. The steady repetition of organized facts, in memorable songs, over a long period of time will lead to lasting knowledge and skills for my children.

All people learn this way. We develop the ability to do new things when we follow a memorable plan. Certainly, we have to be motivated to want to learn, but once the desire is in place, then we are primed for someone to teach us how to do something well. And once we learn how to do something, we carry that skill with us throughout the rest of our lives.

Bible reading is no different. Christians, by virtue of their conversion, often have a hunger for God's word in the days, weeks, and months following their conversion. These times provide a God-given opportunity for church leaders and disciple-makers to help someone learn how to read the Bible well. So what should a good plan look like?

SIMPLE

First, a good Bible reading plan must be simple. While we do not want to create plans that are simplistic, we also want to protect against overly complex systems that invariably communicate that Bible reading is for the professionals. Those who are reading the Bible for the first time will lose heart if our methods are too complex. Remember, it is far easier to add layers of precision to Bible reading as a person becomes increasingly familiar with God's word, but you lose this opportunity if someone gives up in the first place.

MEMORABLE

For plans to work, they must have a certain stickiness to them. For some, acronyms will accomplish this goal (see the S.O.A.P method above). Others may find the arrows memorable. What is true in each case is that the plan can easily be called to mind when someone is sitting down to read the Bible on Monday morning. While a list of 37 hermeneutical principles may be helpful, it is unlikely that average readers will retain these ideas–much less be able to apply them to their personal time with God. In addition, the simplicity and reproducibility of a good model creates a common, shared language among our church members.

In our church, we've created simple book marks of the Seven Arrows and have given them out to our congregation to allow them to have a built-in cheat sheet when they open their Bible. In reality, however, once someone has used the arrows for a few weeks, they will be able to call the arrows to mind quite quickly without the help of the bookmarks. See the downloadable bookmark file at mattrogers.bio if you'd like to use them in your church as well.

REPRODUCIBLE

The stickiness factor aids in reproducibility. Ask anyone who has trained others to do any task–from data entry to lawn mower repair–and you are likely to find that they learned a process for accomplishing the task and are now capable of communicating that process to others. The same is true for spiritual disciplines. As Paul instructed Timothy, we must entrust these things "to faithful men who will be able to teach others also" (2 Tim 2:2).

So, our goal in training Bible readers is not simply to teach them to read the Bible well, but also to teach them so that they can teach others. Thus, our methods should be simple enough for them to sit down with a co-worker or neighbor and work through a passage of Scripture with confidence and clarity. As they do, the word of God moves throughout our communities and disciples are made as a result.

APPLICABLE

Finally, we want to create models that are applicable to all types of situations in which people interact with God's word. Ideally, the ethos of our churches are infused with God's word in a host of contexts, ranging from the proclamation of the word through preaching and teaching, the weekly studies held in small groups, one-on-one discipleship relationships among our members, and each individual believer's personal quiet time. Let's now apply the seven arrows to each of those contexts.

HOW DO YOU APPLY A PLAN?

Application is everything. Models are great, but if our people are not putting the models into practice, then all of our planning is likely to have little effect. Thus, we must see to it that our members have a model and see how to use it in the various facets of their daily lives.

PERSONAL QUIET TIME

The first, and perhaps easiest, context to apply a model like the Seven Arrows is through daily Bible reading. Of course, no model can make up for a lack of discipline or passivity on the part of our people. So, we must pray that God will do what only He can do and incite in our people deep hunger for His word.

When He does, we trust God's word that this word is "living and active, sharper than any two-edged sword, piercing to the division of soul and of spirit, of joints and of marrow, and discerning the thoughts and intentions of the heart" (Heb 4:12). The living word is capable of bringing transformation to all people since "no creature is hidden from His sight" (Heb 4:13). God still speaks and transforms today through His word. So, our models, like Seven Arrows, are a tool by which God's Spirit can bring changes in the lives of those we are called to serve.

The primary place this transformation will happen is in the individual's personal devotions. The Seven Arrows can provide the novice Bible reader with a plan to sit down with their Bibles and a good cup of coffee and hear God speak to them each day. We should exhort our people to begin each day with a set time to meet with the Lord. Awareness of the model and a simple guide, such as the bookmark, can be all they need. Then, we just need to tell them where to begin.

Two options are advisable at this point. First, we might suggest a daily Bible reading plan that would allow them to read through a significant section of the Bible, or the entirety of the Bible, in the course of a year. This plan, while helpful, can often heighten the insecurity of those new to the Bible. Those who have not developed the habit of meeting with God each day may grow discouraged if they fall behind or enter a more challenging section of Scripture. If they are anything like me, they might give up if they hit the month of February and are only on day eleven of their Bible reading plan.

Another approach is to direct them to a specific book of the Bible. This approach would allow them to read through a book at their own pace. Many people who are new to the Bible will assume that they should approach it like another other book and begin at the start, in the book of Genesis. This may be a helpful method for some, but others will likely tap out when they enter the book of Numbers. It is likely that you will grow weary of the consistent repetition and also confused by the vast cultural differences between yourself and the nation of Israel.

Perhaps it would be advisable to ask the Bible reader to begin with one of the Gospels or a small New Testament epistle, like the book of Ephesians. These passages, due to their position in redemptive history, are often easier for Bible readers to understand and apply to their context. Also, Jesus' role in these texts is more overt, leading to a clearer understanding than some Old Testament passages. Once the reader builds confidence in one such book then he or she may be able to enter a more difficult book and handle it well. The book by book study allows the disciple-maker to cater an a la carte reading plan that meets the needs and ability of the Bible reader.

Typically, it is best to use the Seven Arrows on smaller segments of Scripture. Rather than reading one chapter at a time, you could read an individual story. Most English Bibles will help with this task by breaking up the chapters into thematic units under a major heading.

For example,

Matthew 14:1–12   "The Death of John the Baptist"

Matthew 14:13–21   "Jesus Feeds the Five Thousand"

Matthew 14:22–33   "Jesus Walks on the Water"

Matthew 14:34–36   "Jesus Heals the Sick at Gennesaret"

These divisions provide a good guide for bite-sized portion of Bible reading.

One word of caution is necessary. For you to reap the benefits of the Seven Arrows, it is always best to read through books of the Bible in their entirety. Most people erroneously approach the Bible like a dictionary in which you look up a verse and immediately apply it to your life. We feed this faulty notion if we do not train our people to read entire sections of the Bible and trace the authorial intent throughout. This allows the reader to keep the text in its biblical context and fosters a proper understanding of a passage. The best way to do this is to read through one book of the Bible at a time before moving on to another book. This plan will allow you to see the main points the author is making, recognize the way that he develops an argument, and see how he connects the various themes of the book to one another. This does not mean that you have to work through all 66 books in order, but it does mean that you should not read Mark 6, followed by Exodus 32, and then skip to Ephesians 6. This random method of Bible reading will often leave you confused and frustrated.

The Arrows also foster meditation on a biblical text throughout the day. Think of the last time you grilled out with friends. You can always tell the difference in a piece of chicken that has had sauce poured on it while it was on the grill and the same piece of meat that has been marinating for the last 24-hours. The time spent marinating the meat results in a tasty treat.

In the same way, the word of God needs time to marinate in your mind and in your heart. For this to happen, you must do more than simply read a text early in the morning, answer the Seven Arrows, and then move on with the day. Instead, we should remind our people that they should allow God's word to marinate in their minds as they move through the day.

One effective way to do this is to find ways to recall the passage throughout the day. Some may write out the passage on a note card and attach it to their steering wheel or bathroom mirror. Another tool to aid in consistently reflecting on the word is memorization. I know that the word itself strikes fear in the hearts of many, however, memorizing Scripture does not have to be intimidating. We all memorize things continually (like song lyrics). This memorization allows the word to fill the minds and hearts of our people throughout the day. What is critical is that we model the link between one discipline (Bible reading) and other disciplines (Scripture memory, evangelism, or fasting) by showing how growth in one area often enhances another area in need of discipline.

ONE-ON-ONE DISCIPLESHIP

Ideally, the Seven Arrows, or any such Bible reading plan, will be used in a community of believers and not simply by an individual

Christian. It is one thing for a pastor to stand before the congregation and exhort them to read the Bible, explain a plan, and challenge them towards growth in Christ-likeness. It is another thing altogether for pastors to create a culture in which mature Christians take a younger believer under his or her wing and read the Bible together. I also wrote a discipleship workbook, *Aspire*, designed to provide a guide for one-on-one discipleship in the church. *Aspire* is a 15-week study, written in two parts, designed to be used to disciple believers in the local church. Each week's study combines rich theological content and clear practical application in a journal-based format. Ideal for one-on-one discipleship relationships, *Aspire* guides believers towards life-long transformation. You can find it on Amazon or at mattrogers.bio.

We might issue this type of challenge through our sermons each week. There, we can explain the need for one-on-one discipleship and exhort our church to seek out others for the sake of developing these relationships. Some may act. Many will not. For a culture of disciple-making to result, pastors will often have to play the role of E-Harmony at the outset. They will need to approach a seasoned Christian and introduce them to someone in need of discipleship. Armed with a plan like the Seven Arrows, this mature believer can guide the younger disciple towards maturity. Ideally, every new convert or younger believer (either age or maturity) in our churches would be paired with a seasoned Christ-follower for an intentional process of discipleship.

Once the relationship forms, these two people simply need to agree on a book they will read together. By together, I do not mean that you should actually read together in the same room. Instead, they agree upon a section of Scripture, and read it over the course of a given week. Then, they pick a time to meet together to discuss what was read. For example, two people could read the book of Ephesians together. There are approximately seven major headings in chapters 1–3, which would provide a week's worth of daily devotional reading. So, two believers in your church might pair up and read chapter 1–3 over the course of a given week and get together and discuss their answers to the Seven Arrows.

These one-on-one relationships will aid Bible readers in a number of ways. First, it will reassure a novice Bible reader that they are on the right track if they hear their answers confirmed by a more mature believer. Second, these relationships will provide added clarity on the passage, since two believers are more likely see aspects of the text that one person might miss if he or she were reading in isolation. Next, relationships aid in correcting aberrant or heretical ideas. A single Bible reader may concoct a false view of a biblical text, even using the Arrows. When they read in community, however, these ideas are more likely to be challenged and corrected. Finally, these relationships provide a natural context for applying arrows 5 through 7. Bible readers can share the way God's Spirit convicted them of sin or challenged them to obedience, and be held accountable for continued growth in these areas.

One-on-one Bible reading could even be a united church practice. For example, it is common for Christians to seek out a new Bible reading plan at the beginning of a new year or to commit to greater intentionality in the word than they had last year. Knowing this, a pastor could challenge his church to seek out one-on-one discipleship relationships and all read the book of John together. You could even map out a weekly reading plan to keep the discipleship clusters on the same reading pace. This might allow you to sync up the church's reading with a major teaching series you are doing, or simply get everyone studying a book of the Bible that you believe is critical at that juncture in the life of your church.

The spillover of effective Bible reading is not limited to discipleship relationships within our churches, however. It should extend far beyond your closest friends and family. A genuine commitment to being transformed by God's word will raise the spiritual antenna of our people and make them more aware of the work of God in the places they live, work, and play. This may include a random conversation with a stranger in a store check-out line or an extended conversation with a mom while the kids play on the playground. Believers can seek to infuse these relationships with the word of God as they grow in listening to Him speak through His word using an effective model. In time, this will allow our people to speak words of grace and truth to those who are far from Christ.

SMALL GROUPS OR CLASS ROOM SETTINGS

When I planted a church in 2010, I wrote a series of questions based on the sermon from that week to guide small group discussions. My intentions were good–I wanted our people to think about one central idea each week rather than hearing a sermon on one topic and then discussing an unrelated topic in their groups.

This changed when I began to lead my own small group and visit other groups in our church. I was quickly convicted by how much time the group spent discussing the sermon from Sunday and how little time they actually spent reading and discussing the Bible itself. Instead of asking, "What did the biblical author mean when he wrote this passage?" the small groups responded to "What did you guys think about the second point in the sermon?"

About this same time I became increasingly aware of the need that people had for learning how to read the Bible for themselves. Not only were they spending inordinate amounts of time discussing sermons and not the Bible, but I was also missing a prime opportunity equip our people to read the Bible well. The same principle can be at play in Sunday School classrooms or other medium-sized teaching venues. In these settings, people may read secondary commentary on a biblical text and guide their discussions by questions posed by curriculum writers. While helpful, we may be neglecting a prime context where we could train our people to read the Bible for themselves.

So, at The Church at Cherrydale, we made a change. Rather than discussing the sermon from Sunday we began using the Seven Arrows as the basis for all of our small groups. They would take Sunday's text and walk through it using the questions posed by the Arrows. We felt like this process would allow us to leverage our small groups to equip the church to read the Bible well.

We also did one other thing. Rather than discussing the biblical text the week *following* it being preached on a Sunday, we asked our small groups to discuss the passage in the week *prior* to it being preached. We noticed that once a passage has been preached in a sermon it is almost impossible to see the text with fresh eyes. People always read the passage through the lens of the sermon—and then subtly drift back into discussing the sermon more than the biblical text. We wanted to remove this temptation so we asked them to discuss the text before it was preached. This, in our mind, most closely approximates people's experience when they sit down to read the Bible on their couch with a cup of coffee on Monday morning. Over time our prayer was that these questions would become second-nature due to the repetition of their use in our church family. Whether they are used before or after the sermon is not important. What is important is that our people learn to read God's word well.

CLASSES

Classes are important aids in training our churches to read the Bible well. These class can range from Sunday School to medium-sized discipleship courses offered on Sundays or throughout the week. We have used the Seven Arrows to guide a course entitled "How to Read the Bible" since implementing the model. This course, ranging from 12 to 14 weeks, is led by someone who has faithfully discipled others using the model and has utilized it in a small group.

The first week of the course is an introduction to the doctrine of Scripture, in which we affirm a high view of God's word and instruct our members on its centrality to their lives. Over the following seven weeks we take one arrow at a time and discuss the way in which a person might answer that question well. Then, the concluding four to six weeks are spent walking through a short book of the Bible using the arrows. For example, we might guide the group through a discussion of the book of Ruth over four weeks. Each week we would break up into small subgroups, discuss our answers to each arrow, and then come back together as a larger group to compare our answers. This allows all Bible readers to gain confidence and listen to the principles that are guiding others in their answers. Our goal is that these classes provide a crash course in Bible reading for those who are new converts or who are unsure of their ability to read the Bible well. In time, not only do they learn how to do so, but they are equipped to disciple others through one-on-one relationships.

The book, *Seven Arrows: Aiming Bible Readers in the Right Direction*, which I co-authored with Donny Mathis can provide help for such classes. I knew there were weaknesses in the Arrows as a stand alone tool. They provided a clear path, but the path needed some light along the way. This book is an effort to illuminate the path that the Arrows provide. The Arrows force the reader to ask the right questions, but the answers may still be difficult to see at times. For example, how does a reader discern what the text meant to its original readers (Arrow 2)? Or, what if the passage seems to say something about God that doesn't make sense (Arrow 3)?

The answers to these questions often prompt lengthy, academic resources that are seemingly inaccessible to the modern Bible reader. That doesn't have to be the case though. I have watched our congregation, The Church at Cherrydale in Greenville, South Carolina, grow under the teaching of men like Dr. Donny Mathis. We have worked diligently to take the simple Arrows that I developed and teach our congregation to be effective Bible-readers.

For that reason, I asked Donny to help me turn this tool into a simple book designed to provide increased light to the Arrows and clarify how a reader should go about answering those questions properly. This task serves as the basis of Donny's training and vocation. As a graduate of The Southern Baptist Theological Seminary with a PhD in New Testament and a professor of Greek, Hermeneutics, and New Testament among other things, he is trained to speak to this issue well. However, he is far from an ivory tower theologian. His greatest strength is that he is a faithful member of our local church, where he also serves as a lay elder. From this position, he is able to provide practical tools that can aid anyone seeking to read and understand the Bible better and not simply those seeking out a theological degree. You can find our book on Amazon or at mattrogers.bio.

SERMONS

The weekly sermon provides one final way to use a model like Seven Arrows in your church. The hard work of the sermon for many of us may not be the complexity required to study the text, discern the author's meaning, and package the sermon outline together into a compelling manuscript. What may be the most challenging work is taking the complex, theological ideas and making them simple for the congregation and showing how these ideas are clearly discerned from a study of the biblical text itself. If the congregation hears the preacher flexing his theological muscles or waxing eloquently about secondary minutia unrelated to the text, they are unlikely to learn how to study the passage for themselves. And, though not intentionally, the pastor may be contributing to their insecurity regarding their own ability to read and understand the Bible.

Therefore, a preacher can make their Bible study model overt in their weekly preaching. Clearly, this does not mean that each sermon is outlined around the Seven Arrows, nor that the pastor should use each of the questions in every sermon. However, a preacher should answer each of the arrows every week. Each sermon should explain the authors' intent, the cultural context, how God is seen and sin is exposed, what people should do, how they should love, and how they should pray.

At times, it may be appropriate for the pastor to be explicit by asking and answering one of the questions posed by the Arrows. For example, if a pastor were teaching on the golden calf episode from Exodus 32, he may answer Arrow 3 by showing how God's love and steadfast faithfulness is seen through the passage. In time, as the church grows more familiar with a model like the Seven Arrows, they will not have to hear the question mentioned in the sermon to notice that the pastor is providing an answer to a certain Arrow's question.

A third area of your life where you should see growth as a result of using the Seven Arrows is in your time listening to sermons or other forms of Bible teaching. We have sought to free you from an over-dependence on sermons and Bible teaching and to show you that you can do much of that work on your own. This goal, however, is not intended to devalue sermons. In fact, daily and consistent Bible intake should make you a better listener during sermons and Bible studies. Our prayer is that you would act like the Bereans, who in Acts 17 diligently searched the Scriptures after hearing Paul and Silas teach in order to confirm the things they had heard.

If you know the passage your pastor will be preaching from each Sunday, then you can work through the text using Seven Arrows prior to hearing the sermon. This practice will allow you to come to the sermon with a soft heart that has already been broken by the message of the passage in question. It can also be a useful tool in confirming your study throughout the week. Imagine your joy if you were able to listen to a sermon and think, *Yeah. That's exactly what I thought this week!* Typically, your pastor will still be able to provide depth and clarity to the text that you may not have seen, but if you work through the text effectively, you will have done much of the work prior to the sermon and will be encouraged by the fruit of your study.

Before long, you may find that you are more confident in teaching the Bible to others as well. Often, people think that a seminary degree is required in order to lead a Bible study or small group at their local church. This, however, is not the case. A person who studies the Bible daily using Seven Arrows will quickly find that he is capable of teaching others through books of the Bible. Do not be surprised if God uses this process to call you into higher levels of leadership in your local church than you currently hold.

A GUIDE FOR USING THE ARROWS

There is no perfect method. The Seven Arrows are merely a guide, but I believe it is a very helpful guide for teaching people to read the Bible well. It is designed to be practical and leave you with a plan for sitting down with your Bible, reading through any book, understanding what you've read, and being able to apply it to your life. Now, let's look at a few examples from various genres of Scripture to show how I would use the arrows. Think of this as eavesdropping on my quiet time as I journal using the Seven Arrows to study the Bible.

OLD TESTAMENT NARRATIVE

And when the LORD your God brings you into the land that he swore to your fathers, to Abraham, to Isaac, and to Jacob, to give you—with great and good cities that you did not build, and houses full of all good things that you did not fill, and cisterns that you did not dig, and vineyards and olive trees that you did not plant—and when you eat and are full, then take care lest you forget the LORD, who brought you out of the land of Egypt, out of the house of slavery. It is the LORD your God you shall fear. Him you shall serve and by his name you shall swear. You shall not go after other gods, the gods of the peoples who are around you—for the LORD your God in your midst is a jealous God—lest the anger of the LORD your God be kindled against you, and he destroy you from off the face of the earth.

– Deuteronomy 6:10-15 ESV

What does this
passage say?

God warned the nation that they would be tempted to forget about him when they took up residence in the promised land because of the vast provision of God they would find there.

What did this passage mean
to its original audience?

Having seen their parents die in the wilderness and spent years wandering themselves, the people would have likely assumed they would not forget God who had so clearly brought them into the land.

What does this passage
tell us about God?

God is faithful to his people, though he knows that they will, in fact, forget him and take his blessings for granted.

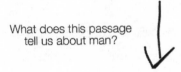

What does this passage
tell us about man?

People are forgetful. Particularly when they have ample provision and peace, all people are prone to forget about God and his grace that has given them those good gifts.

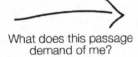

What does this passage
demand of me?

I, too, am the unworthy recipient of much grace from God's hand and if I am not careful I will forget to live in constant thanksgiving to God. I must renounce my idols and live in humble praise to God.

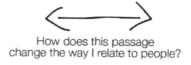

How does this passage
change the way I relate to people?

Many around me live in luxury, blinding them to their need for
God and filling their life with idols. I should pray that God would
use my life as an example of dependence on God and not myself.

How does this passage
prompt me to pray?

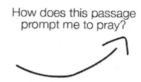

God, I thank you for your faithfulness to your people. As I saw
today, you kept your promises to the nation of Israel, even though
you knew they would forget about you. Help me, today, to keep you
before me throughout the day. May your Spirit guide me to think
on you, to love you, to follow you, and to shun the idols that my
heart often craves.

PROPHECY

And I heard the voice of the Lord saying, "Whom shall
I send, and who will go for us?" Then I said, "Here I
am! Send me." And he said, "Go, and say to this people: "'Keep on hearing, but do not understand; keep
on seeing, but do not perceive.' Make the heart of
this people dull, and their ears heavy, and blind their
eyes; lest they see with their eyes, and hear with their

ears, and understand with their hearts, and turn and be healed." Then I said, "How long, O Lord?" And he said: "Until cities lie waste without inhabitant, and houses without people, and the land is a desolate waste, and the LORD removes people far away, and the forsaken places are many in the midst of the land. And though a tenth remain in it, it will be burned again, like a terebinth or an oak, whose stump remains when it is felled." The holy seed is its stump.

–Isaiah 6:8-13 ESV

What does this
passage say?

After seeing God in all of His glory, Isaiah is commissioned to take God's message to a group of people who would not listen or repent as a result of his message.

What did this passage mean
to its original audience?

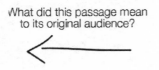

Isaiah was compelled by the holiness of God to do whatever he was asked to do. However, he would have surely been discouraged by the fact that God told him ahead of time that the people would not heed his warning and that he would have to continue to proclaim the message until their destruction.

What does this passage tell us about God?

God continues to proclaim His word to those who will ultimately reject Him and face his judgment.

What does this passage tell us about man?

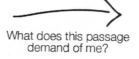

The hard-heart of man leads many to fail to listen to the warnings of God's appointed messengers. This does not mean that God's people should not continue to proclaim His word.

What does this passage demand of me?

I must be bold to proclaim the word of God to my friends, family, neighbors, and co-workers, even if they do not listen. God is worthy of my ultimate allegiance regardless of what others may say.

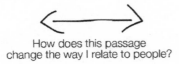

How does this passage
change the way I relate to people?

I should pray and plead with others and trust that God is the only one who can change their hearts.

How does this passage
prompt me to pray?

God, you are holy. Like Isaiah, I have seen your holiness and been commissioned by You to be Your ambassador to a lost world. Empower me to speak Your word to those You put in my path. Protect me from the fear of man that would cause me to shy away from the good work You have called me to.

GOSPELS

Now as they went on their way, Jesus entered a village. And a woman named Martha welcomed him into her house. And she had a sister called Mary, who sat at the Lord's feet and listened to his teaching. But Martha was distracted with much serving. And she went up to him and said, "Lord, do you not care that my sister has left me to serve alone? Tell her then to help me." But the Lord answered her, "Martha, Martha, you are anxious and troubled about many things, but one thing is necessary. Mary has chosen the good portion, which will not be taken away from her."

– Luke 10:38-42 ESV

What does this
passage say?

Jesus commends Mary for listening to His teaching, in contrast to Martha who is busy attending to the details of life.

What did this passage mean
to its original audience?

Martha was seemingly doing good work as she sought to serve Jesus and provide for His needs. Mary, instead, focused her attention on learning from Jesus and treasuring His company. The person who seemed lazy was, in fact, making the wise choice.

What does this passage
tell us about God?

God wants the undivided attention of His children.

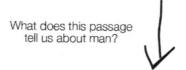

What does this passage
tell us about man?

People are prone to religious activities rather than the worship of God. We often seek to do things for God rather than treasure His presence in our lives.

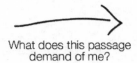

What does this passage
demand of me?

I must seek to sit at Jesus' feet, hear from Him, and worship Him well. Rather than busying my life with activity, I must learn to rest and find joy in God's nearness in my life.

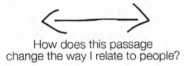

How does this passage
change the way I relate to people?

I should work to develop a culture in my home and in my church that is content with Jesus alone. I should encourage others to treasure Jesus above all things, even the good things with which we fill our lives.

How does this passage
prompt me to pray?

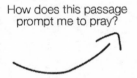

God, you have been gracious in calling me into relationship with You. You have come near to me, even though I do not deserve to have a right relationship with You. Forgive me for neglecting You, even when I think that I am doing good things. Help me to have a heart like Mary that would desire nothing more than to sit in Your presence.

LETTERS

And you were dead in the trespasses and sins in which you once walked, following the course of this world, following the prince of the power of the air, the spirit that is now at work in the sons of disobedience—among whom we all once lived in the passions of our flesh, carrying out the desires of the body and the mind, and were by nature children of wrath, like the rest of mankind. But God, being rich in mercy, because of the great love with which he loved us, even when we were dead in our trespasses, made us alive together with Christ—by grace you have been saved—and raised us up with him and seated us with him in the heavenly places in Christ Jesus, so that in the coming ages he might show the immeasurable riches of his grace in kindness toward us in Christ Jesus. For by grace you have been saved through faith. And this is not your own doing; it is the gift of God, not a result of works, so that no one may boast. For we are his workmanship, created in Christ Jesus for good works, which God prepared beforehand, that we should walk in them.

– Ephesians 2:1-10 ESV

What does this
passage say?

All people are dead in sin, separated from God, and rightful objects of His wrath, but God loved His children, sent Jesus to pay the price for their sin, and graciously saved them from God's judgment.

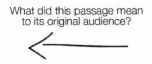

What did this passage mean
to its original audience?

The Ephesian church would have been reminded of the message of the gospel and the hope that is theirs by virtue of Jesus' work.

What does this passage
tell us about God?

God is rich in grace and mercy and acted on behalf of fallen sinners to do for them by grace what they could never do on their own.

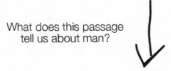

What does this passage
tell us about man?

Apart from God's grace, all people are hopeless and helpless. Because of God's grace, those same people can be given life and give their lives away to the good works God has prepared for them.

What does this passage
demand of me?

I should praise God for His kindness in Christ Jesus and find joy in the knowledge that I am saved by grace apart from my works.

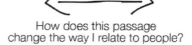

How does this passage
change the way I relate to people?

I should pray that God would do what only He can do and save those who are dead in sin. In turn, I should point others to the hope of the gospel found only through Jesus Christ.

How does this passage
prompt me to pray?

God, you saved me when I was helplessly dead in my sin. Had You not acted, I was doomed. But, because You have acted I am the recipient of Your grace and given the eternal riches of Christ. I praise You that I am raised and seated with Christ and that my eternal fate is secure.

CONCLUSION

As leaders in God's church, we long to be faithful and fruitful in our work to equip God's people. There is no greater equipping work than that of training our people to read God's word well. My prayer is that you would seek out a model, put it in practice, and trust God to produce life-transformation in those you are called to serve. I trust that the fruit of our labor will produce an army of God's people who will be unleashed on a disciple-making mission, which will lead to awestruck, life-encompassing worship as they are transformed by God's word. I also pray that this version of *Pastor's Notes* has been helpful to you as you seek to lead God's church. In the months and years ahead, I plan to write a number of other volumes in this series. Come back to mattrogers.bio for updates on the newest editions of these resources. I trust that God will multiply my meagre efforts to produce lasting fruit in the churches we lead.

ABOUT THE AUTHOR

Matt Rogers lives in Greenville, South Carolina with his wife, Sarah, and their four children where he serves as one of the elders of The Church at Cherrydale (www.tccherrydale.com). His teaching and writing ministry is birthed out of his passion to equip the church to mature as worshippers of God. Matt completed his undergraduate education at Furman University (BA in Psychology) and graduate studies at Gordon-Conwell Theological Seminary (MA in Counseling) and Southeastern Baptist Theological Seminary (MDiv in Pastoral Ministry; PhD in Applied Theology). Matt speaks throughout North America and is the author of *Aspire: Developing and Deploying Disciples in the Church and For the Church* and *Mergers: Combining Churches to Multiply Disciples*. Follow Matt on Twitter @mattrogers_ or online at mattrogers.bio.

Made in the USA
Middletown, DE
25 June 2016